To: Tony

Never say never.

4.10.03

NEVER SAY NEVER

by Doug Flutie

with Greg Brown

Illustrations by Doug Keith

Taylor Trade Publishing
Dallas, Texas

Greg Brown has been involved in sports for thirty years as an athlete and award-winning sportswriter. Brown started his Positively For Kids series after he was unable to find sports books that taught life lessons for his own children. Doug's book is the 16th in the series. Brown regularly speaks at schools and may be reached at greg@PositivelyForKids.com. He lives in Bothell, Washington, with his wife, Stacy, and two children, Lauren and Benji.

Doug Keith has provided illustrations for national magazines such as *Sports Illustrated for Kids*, greeting cards, and books. Keith may be reached at his Internet address: atozdk@aol.com.

All photos courtesy of Doug Flutie and family except the following:

AllSport: 3 left, 5 left, 29 top left, 34 bottom, 35, 38 right. AP/Wide World: 3 right, 4 right center, 5 right, 25, 27 top and bottom left, 28 top, 29 top right and bottom left, 32 top, 34 top, 36 top left, 37 top left, 38 left, 40. Greg Brown: 16 lower left, 36 top right, two-page spread. CP Picture Archive/Dave Buston: 31. Tom DiPace: 28 bottom, 39. The Doug Flutie Jr. Foundation for Autism: 37 top right. Richard Flutie: 6 bottom, 7, 9, 10, 11, 12 bottom, 14, 16 top, 18, 19, 21, 26 top right. William Flutie: 12 top. C. J. Gunther/SIPA: 33 top. PLB Sports: 37 bottom right. John Sokolowski: 4 far left. *Sports Illustrated:* 22, 23, 24 bottom right and top left, 27 bottom right, 30 bottom, 32 bottom. *Vancouver Sun*/Jeff Vinnick: 30 top. Tom Wolf: 33 bottom.

A portion of the proceeds from this book will be donated to the Doug Flutie, Jr. Foundation for Autism, a member of the Giving Back Fund's Family of Charities. To learn more about the foundation on the Internet, go to:
www.dougflutie.org

Copyright © 2000 by Doug Flutie and Greg Brown

Designed by Steve Willgren

Published by Taylor Publishing Company
1550 West Mockingbird Lane
Dallas, Texas 75235
www.taylorpub.com

Library of Congress Cataloging-in-Publication Data is available.

Printed in the United States of America

10 9 8 7 6 5 4 3 2 1

Hi. I'm Doug Flutie.
I have played professional football in three decades, for three different leagues, and on seven different teams, including three National Football League teams.

Not bad for a 5-foot 9¾-inch guy the so-called experts said isn't tall enough to play quarterback.

Throughout my professional career I've been looked down upon because of my size. I've been told I'll never make it. I've been teased by team-mates and mocked by the media.

I've experienced many things thanks to football. I've written this book to share some of those lessons with you.

My career has been a wild ride.

I've met many interesting people and made tremendous friends. Owners have paid me a lot of money to play on their teams.

I have felt the elation of winning three Canadian Football League championships, known as the Grey Cup. I've also felt the despair of losing National Football League playoff games.

I've been on the winning and losing sides of two famous football games that ended on dramatic, unbelievable plays.

Me with Ronald Reagan ...

... Heather Locklear and Jon BonJovi ...

... and Mary Lou Retton and Bob Hope.

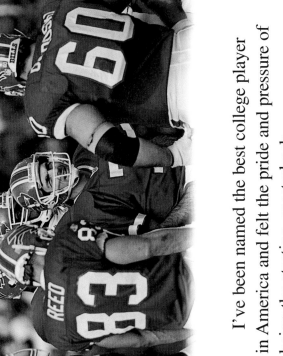

I've been named the best college player in America and felt the pride and pressure of being the starting quarterback.

I also know what it's like to be unwanted. I have been cut by a team and benched by two coaches.

I've known fame, and I've felt forgotten. I might be the shortest player on the field, but I'm never the smallest. I neither listen to nor believe negative comments about me. Through it all, no matter what people say, no matter what happens, I never believe I'm defeated. I never say never.

Edward Flutie (left).

Doug.

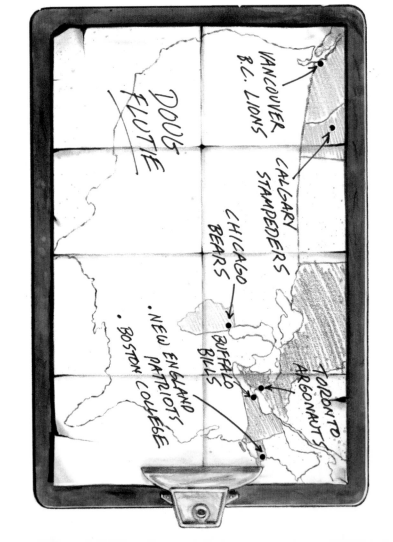

DOUG FLUTIE

VANCOUVER B.C. LIONS

CALGARY STAMPEDERS

CHICAGO BEARS

BUFFALO BILLS

NEW ENGLAND PATRIOTS

BOSTON COLLEGE

TORONTO ARGONAUTS

"You'll never play football," my grandfather ruled as my father, Richard, grew up.

You see, Edward Flutie played football in the days without facemasks and broke his nose several times. He figured the rough sport wasn't worth it and wanted something better for his son. So my dad never played football. He did play some basketball and golf in high school, as did my mother. Music is what motivated my dad. He played the piano and organ and dreamed about being a professional musician. He even started his own orchestra in Baltimore, Maryland, where I was born in a medium-income suburban neighborhood. My earliest memories are of playing tackle football with my brothers and sister in our small Baltimore row house's chain-link-fenced backyard.

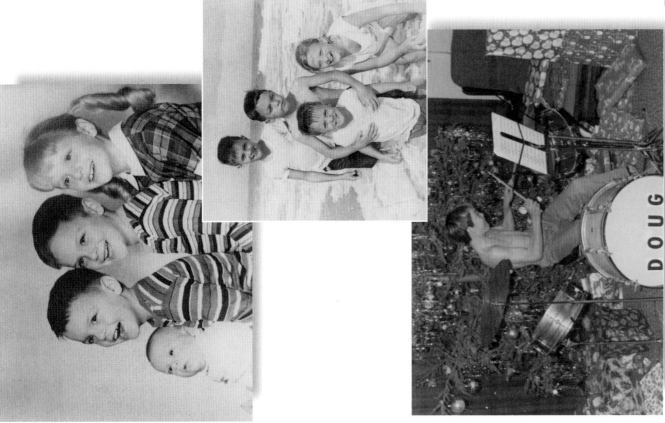

My dad attended Dickinson College in Carlisle, Pennsylvania, and Johns Hopkins University at night. We lived paycheck to paycheck. I became a fan of the Baltimore Orioles and the Baltimore Colts. I went to some of their games. I wore No. 22 many years because O's pitcher Jim Palmer had that number, and I looked up to him as a player.

When I turned six we moved to Melbourne Beach, Florida, where Dad found work as a scanning electron microscopist. My parents introduced us to music at early ages, hoping we might someday form a Flutie family band. I started with the trumpet and learned to read music. Later, at age ten, I switched to the drums after receiving a set at Christmas. I loved pounding away for hours on our back porch. I still love playing the drums. Darren, my younger brother, and I started the Flutie Brothers band back in 1992. I play the drums and Darren plays guitar. Three other guys are in the band with us. We perform about ten times a year and have cut two rock-and-roll CDs.

I fell in love with sports before I ever played on a team. I'd roll out of bed and jump into a pair of shorts and be dressed for the day. We'd play yard sports barefooted all day in the Florida sunshine.

Around the house I constantly thought up new games to play. Hallway football, ten ball (baseball with a tennis ball), fastpitch baseball (pitching into a hockey net), and cup baseball were all fun. Cup baseball evolved into a family favorite indoor game. We'd push two paper cups together and hit the paper "ball" with our hand. Sometimes our roughhousing got out of control, and we'd get in trouble for breaking things. We once busted our clock three times in three weeks.

I've always been fascinated by alligators. I had a brush with one at age ten in Florida. I was playing golf with my older brother, Bill. I hit a ball about twenty feet away from a pond. I pulled out my club and hit the ball. As I slid my club back into my golf bag and started to walk, I noticed a gator two club-lengths away resting in the grass. Fortunately the alligator never moved. I sure did after seeing it.

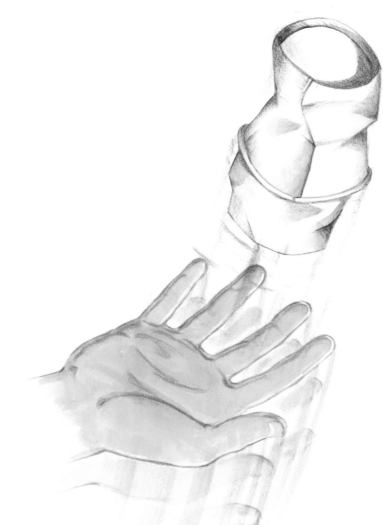

The organized sports bug crawled into our Florida home when Bill decided he wanted to try Little League baseball.

My parents embraced Little League and got involved. Today, the Melbourne Beach Little League park is called "Flutie Athletic Complex." It honors my family for devoting countless hours to running the park.

Darren, my sister Denise, and I spent our weekends watching Bill play baseball. We lived at the ballpark during the season and seemingly ate hot dogs and popcorn for all three meals.

I started Little League baseball at age seven, unsure of myself. I'll admit baseball scared me at first. When I went to the plate that year, the bat stayed on my shoulder as I stood as still as a tree. I hoped for a walk every time.

The next year, I learned good things happen when you swing. I started hitting the ball, even smashing a few home runs. I played shortstop and pitcher. Dad built a pitcher's mound and target in our backyard, and I threw thousands of balls through an elastic target over a home-made home plate. My baseball skills improved. I made the all-star team as a twelve-year-old.

I showed athletic creativity even then. In an all-star tournament game, I got the final out of an inning at short-stop by faking a throw to first and then diving to second base to tag out a runner.

I found new ways to do things in youth football, too. I started playing football at age eight.

I figured out how I could score when our team kicked off. I'd run down and take the ball from the runner and keep on running the other way for a touchdown.

I did it on the first try. I became so good at stealing the ball from runners that referees often needed a timeout to figure out what happened.

I tried quarterback but found it boring to just hand off the ball. I loved playing running back and defense. None of my youth football teams won more than three games in a season.

In baseball and basketball, we went undefeated and won some championships. To me, playing was everything. Not even injuries could stop me.

I broke my nose in Little League when a thrown ball hit me in the face. I played the next day.

I cracked a bone in my left foot and wore a walking cast for two weeks at the end of a football season. I convinced my doctor to take it off so I could play in an all-star football game. I couldn't run well, so they played me at defensive line—and I collected two sacks!

During youth basketball, I broke a finger on my right hand. I played with a splint and learned to shoot left-handed.

I enjoy talking sports almost as much as playing. After youth games, I talked with my family about the game. The whole game. Every play.

I still love talking sports. My brothers and I spent hours talking about freak plays and dreaming up weird endings to contests.

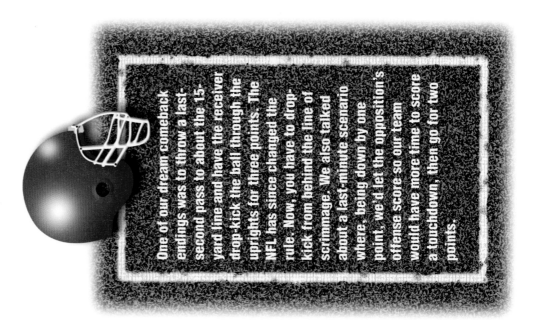

One of our dream comeback endings was to throw a last-second pass to about the 15-yard line and have the receiver drop-kick the ball through the uprights for three points. The NFL has since changed the rule. Now, you have to drop-kick from behind the line of scrimmage. We also talked about a last-minute scenario where, being down by one point, we'd let the opposition's offense score so our team would have more time to score a touchdown, then go for two points.

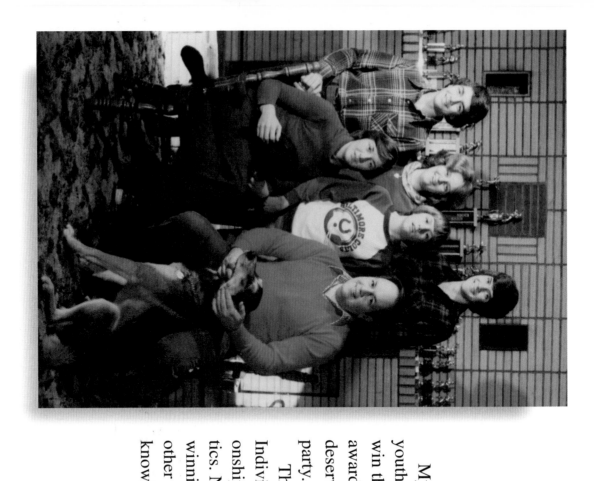

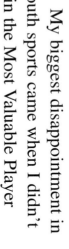

My biggest disappointment in youth sports came when I didn't win the Most Valuable Player award on my sixth-grade football team. I thought I deserved it, but I held in my reaction during our team party.

Throughout the years I've won many awards. Individual awards are nice, but I'll take team championships any day. I used to measure myself by my statistics. Not anymore. Numbers have nothing to do with winning. I can have a great game and lousy stats or the other way around. I play for the satisfaction of winning, knowing I tried my best until the end.

In school, I shined in math.

When I went to the grocery store with Mom during elementary school, I could add the total of our groceries in my head before we got to the checkout stand.

I frustrated my math teachers, however, because during math tests I'd write down just the answer. Teachers wanted to see my equations on paper, but I did it all in my head.

I worked hard at school. I didn't enjoy home-work; I just knew it had to be done.

845+904=1,749   712x33=23,496
300X154=46,200
113x254=28,702   905+355=1,260
425÷17=25
315+475+125=915
895x224=200,480   375÷25=15
595÷17=35   265+300+465=1,030

I had no idea what to expect when Dad's job change moved our family in the middle of the school year up the East Coast to a small town eighteen miles outside of Boston. Dad drove directly to the local newspaper and asked the sportswriter which of the surrounding towns had the best sports tradition. That's how he picked Natick. Moving during the spring quarter wasn't easy.

Some bullies picked on the new kid in town for awhile. A ninth grader followed me into the school bathroom once and tackled me to the ground for no reason. Thanks to sports, I made plenty of friends. Summer baseball teams were picked by then, so Dad formed a team of my brothers and me and players no other coaches wanted. Our team showed that you can never count out players with heart. We surprised everyone by making it to the league championship game.

Even though he had never done it before, Coach Buschenfeldt allowed me to call my own plays.

I proved I could handle it, and the experience gave me an advanced feel for the game. Buschenfeldt told the high school coaches about me.

Our family home in Natick.

Natick didn't have football for my age that first fall. So, once again, Dad helped organize a team. I started playing quarterback full time and loved throwing.

In ninth grade, I won the starting quarterback job at our junior high, the Coolidge Cougars. Coach Kirk Buschenfeldt saw immediately that I had a head for the game.

My sophomore season in high school taught me to never turn down a chance, no matter how slim, because one chance can lead to another.

I hoped to play on the varsity football team with my older brother, Bill, a senior, earned the starting quarterback job with a perfect quarterback body at 6-foot-3. Coaches gave me a chance at defensive back. It didn't matter to me where I played. I even became a kicker and punt returner.

I did play quarterback on the junior-varsity team and had some eye-catching passing games. The coaches took notice.

After five games our varsity team was 3–2 and struggling offensively. The next Monday our JV team scored 50 points with a strong passing attack. The next day Coach Tom Lamb shocked many by replacing Bill at starting quarterback with a sophomore—me. Bill graciously agreed to change positions to wide receiver. It did not matter to us who played quarterback. We both just wanted to be on the field.

"People would say, if Doug only had my height, I'd say, if I only had Doug's talent, his arm strength, and quickness. He had that something special about him."

—Bill, who played for Brown University and graduated with an electrical engineering degree

Fans probably wondered why the coaches didn't yank me off the field during the first half of my first varsity start at quarterback. I threw four interceptions in the first two quarters. The start to anything is never as important as the finish, though. In the second half, I threw three touchdowns, all to Bill, and we won.

Our team finished strong, winning the rest of our games. Bill and I never left the field. We had a blast playing together. We won a game on a last-second 38-yard field goal—on my first career field goal try. Bill was the holder.

The high school state championship game in Massachusetts is called "The Super Bowl." Natick never played in the Super Bowl the three seasons I quarterbacked the team. Two years after I left, however, Natick High won back-to-back Super Bowls with my brother Darren at running back.

In my three seasons, Natick went 8–2, 7–3, and 8–2. We had great comeback wins and some crushing losses. Twice I made the all-state football team, once as a quarterback and once as a defensive back.

I also played basketball, the sport I love the most, and baseball in high school.

My sophomore year I didn't play baseball. Our family ran short of money that spring, and our phone was turned off. So I quit baseball to work at an ice cream shop. I needed a phone to talk to my girlfriend.

During high school, I was a shy kid outside of sports. I never talked back to teachers. I never swore. I never drank alcohol (to this day I've never had a beer). I never smoked. I stayed out of trouble. By my senior year I made the honor society with straight As.

I never felt pressure to try anything. My friends respected my decision and didn't bother me about it.

What terrified me the most in high school was the school dances. You'd think because I love music that I'd enjoy dancing. I didn't.

At the end of my sophomore year, I started dating Laurie Fortier. We met in homeroom. We dated through the rest of high school. She taught me how to move to music, and we've been dancing ever since.

The recruiting dance started early for me. Coaches came to watch me play during my senior year. I never worried about my height until college coaches started talking to me. One coach from Ohio State told me bluntly, "Let's face it, you're not going to be a Division I quarterback."

So many people told me that, I started to believe them. There are times when you shouldn't believe the experts.

Only one Division I college football team—Boston College—offered me a football scholarship. By the time new head coach Jack Bicknell took over, BC's top two quarterback prospects had gone elsewhere. I was their third choice. Our whole recruiting class was dubbed "The Class Nobody Wanted."

I half expected to be moved to defense or wide receiver when I arrived at Boston College for pre-season workouts. Secretly, I felt outclassed by the taller quarterbacks and had my doubts if I would ever throw the ball for BC. I started out ninth on the quarterback depth chart.

By the time the season started, I moved up to fourth-string quarterback, high enough to run the plays of the scout team (which prepares the defense by running the opponents' plays in practice). Once the season started, I did not practice one down with our real offense the first three weeks.

After the third week, I decided I would ask the coaches to move me to a new position after the week-end game.

That week we played at No. 2-ranked Penn State. We were no match and trailed 38–0 in the final quarter. After using all our other quarterbacks, the coaches said, "Let's give the kid a chance."

It didn't matter that it was garbage time in a lopsided game. I played as if we were tied and drove us down the field for a touchdown. Never say never means fighting until your last play, no matter the score, and finding victories inside defeat.

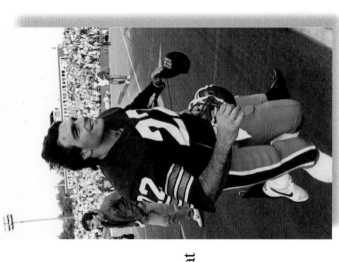

In a game against Penn State, Doug threw for 540 yards, but BC lost thanks to six turnovers. Doug finished third in Heisman Trophy voting, which names the outstanding college football player of the year.

I became the starter, and we finished the season winning four of our last six games, including a near upset of No. 2 Pittsburgh and Dan Marino.

After a 5–6 season, we started seeing winners when we looked in the mirror. That second season we broke the chokehold of team history. We became the first Boston College team to play in a bowl game in forty years.

My junior season brought more attention to our team and me. We moved into the Top Twenty rankings. I appeared on magazine covers and TV shows. We earned a second straight bowl trip, but lost a second time.

That season, my younger brother Darren had an outstanding senior year at Natick High and signed to play at Boston College. I couldn't wait to throw a pass to my brother in a BC game.

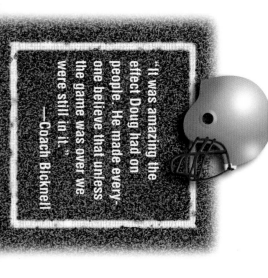

"It was amazing the effect Doug had on people. He made every-one believe that unless the game was over we were still in it."

—Coach Bicknell

Darren caught plenty of passes my senior year. After a 4–0 start, we dreamed of a national championship, but close losses to West Virginia and Penn State broke our hearts. By the time we played the University of Miami, the defending national champions, not much rested on the game played the day after Thanksgiving 1984. We were assured a trip to the Cotton Bowl and the Heisman Trophy voting was complete.

Still, both teams played an all-out never-quit air battle. We trailed 45–41 with 28 seconds left with the ball at our own 20. With six seconds left, we were at the Miami 48. I calmly called a 55 Flood Trip in the huddle. We practiced it every Thursday—a long, high pass that you pray is tipped into the hands of one of your guys, which is why it's called a Hail Mary pass.

It's amazing how many people still want to talk about "The Pass." People always want to tell me where they were when they saw it. When I see the highlight on TV, it brings a smile to my face every time. Several years ago, Gerard and I reenacted the play during a banquet in a massive ballroom. The pass went over chandeliers and dinner tables without breaking a plate, glass, or bone. We were more nervous about that pass than the real one.

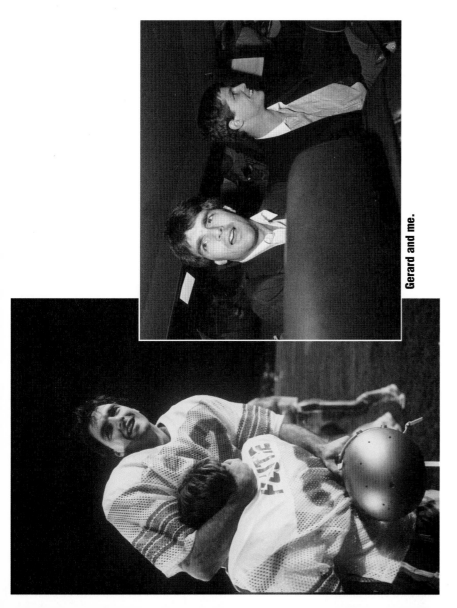

Gerard and me.

Three receivers lined up on the right side and ran toward the end zone. I rolled right to buy some time and let fly a pass that flew 65 yards in the air and just over the heads of the defenders, who probably thought I could not throw it that far. My friend Gerard Phelan pulled it down amid three or four Miami defenders, trapping the ball against his thigh as he landed. I didn't even know it was a touchdown until I saw the referees raise their arms. I found out Phelan made the heroic catch when I got to the locker room.

The comeback victory became magnified because it seemed everyone in the country watched it on TV. We were the only game on TV that night. My life changed from that moment. Suddenly, everyone wanted to talk to me and everyone knew my name.

Awards
- 1984 Heisman Trophy winner
- First major college quarterback to surpass 10,000 career passing yards (10,579) and first to break 11,000 total offense yards (11,054)
- Consensus All-America First Team
- United Press International and Sporting News' "Player of the Year" honors

Game Highlights
- Two touchdown passes on fourth-down plays, led the Eagles to a 38-31 comeback win over the Alabama Crimson Tide at Birmingham
- A record-setting six touchdown passes in a 52-20 romp over North Carolina
- Passed for more yards against a single opponent than any other player in college history: 1,420 vs Penn State Nittany Lions (135 in his first freshman game, 520 in 1982, 380 in 1983, and 447 in 1984)

Academic Highlights
- Chosen as a recipient of a National Football Foundation post-graduate scholarship, and was nominated by Boston College for a Rhodes Scholarship

After our final regular-season game, my parents, Laurie, and I caught a flight to New York for the Heisman Trophy award ceremony. A helicopter took Laurie and me from the airport to downtown. On the way, our pilot asked air traffic control if he could take "Doug Flutie for a tour of New York."

The controller said, "Doug Flutie can go anywhere he wants." I felt on top of the world.

That evening New York's Downtown Athletic Club named me the outstanding college player in America for 1984. I finished my college career with a Cotton Bowl victory over Houston. I wanted that win more than the Heisman. Our team finished fifth in the national rankings, all from the class nobody wanted.

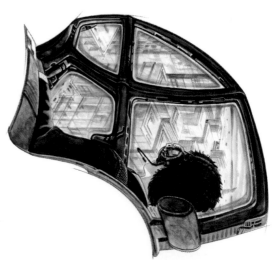

I knew I wanted to spend the rest of my life with Laurie, so on Christmas morning of my senior year in college I gave her a small box to open. She opened the box to find an engagement ring. We were married that summer. The strangest thing about the wedding was there were so many people I didn't know.

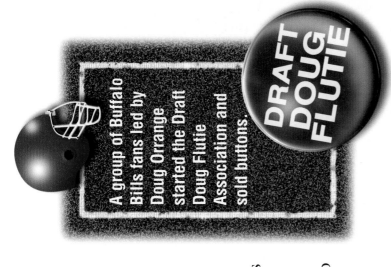

A group of Buffalo Bills fans led by Doug Orrange started the Draft Doug Flutie Association and sold buttons.

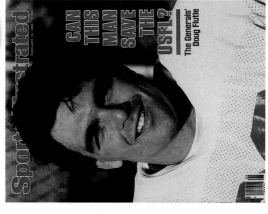

Despite winning the Heisman and setting nine NCAA records, many debated if I could be an NFL quarterback because of my height. Ironically, the Buffalo Bills had the first draft pick but never made a serious offer to me. Instead, New York real estate investor Donald Trump offered me $8 million to join the startup United States Football League, which played its games in the spring. Many great NFL players started in the USFL, including Steve Young, Jim Kelly, and Reggie White. I played one season for the New Jersey Generals, with moderate success until White fell on my left shoulder and ended my season early. The league folded after my first season.

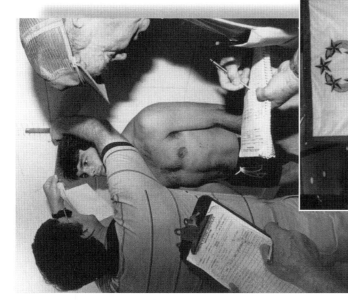

Many USFL players immediately were picked up by NFL teams. My agent found some interest, but no offers came. I waited and waited. I went back to school and earned my degree in communications.

Halfway into the 1986 season, the defending Super Bowl-champion Chicago Bears wanted me as a backup quarterback for injury-prone Jim McMahon. I couldn't believe my good fortune—the Bears and Walter Payton!

The first day I arrived, however, I felt teammate tension. McMahon made it clear he didn't want me around. He openly campaigned against me, calling me "America's Midget" and playing pranks on me.

I never let teasing keep me from my goals. Most who cut down others do it out of frustration or their own insecurity. Never play that game.

Many players, including Payton, supported me. Most importantly, Coach Mike Ditka believed in me.

I played in a handful of games after an injury ended McMahon's season. I won my first start, which earned respect from my teammates. We made the playoffs, and I got the start. I did not play well and neither did our team; we lost to Washington. Going from Super Bowl champions to first-round losers doesn't cut it in the NFL. I became a target of finger pointing.

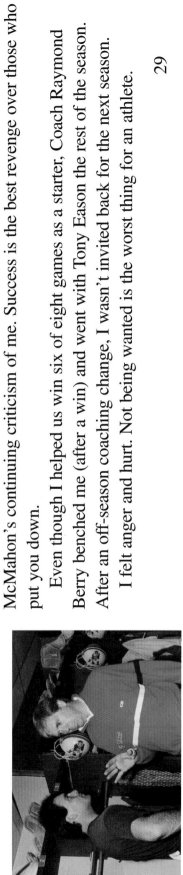

A players' strike wiped out most of the next season, which created a new opportunity. The Bears traded me to the New England Patriots late in the year.

I spent two seasons in my home state with mixed results. The best part was that Laurie and I lived in Natick the whole season and were around family and friends. Natick is still my home.

I showed flashes of my talent in my second season as a Patriot. One week I was the NFL Player of the Week. Later, I led a 30–7 win over Chicago to silence McMahon's continuing criticism of me. Success is the best revenge over those who put you down.

Even though I helped us win six of eight games as a starter, Coach Raymond Berry benched me (after a win) and went with Tony Eason the rest of the season. After an off-season coaching change, I wasn't invited back for the next season. I felt anger and hurt. Not being wanted is the worst thing for an athlete.

My NFL options ran short. So I took an offer to play in Canada with the B.C. Lions, in Vancouver, British Columbia. I didn't know much about the CFL, which has a wider field, deeper end zones, and three plays to make a first down instead of four, among other differences.

The CFL is not as glamorous as the NFL. The crowds aren't as big and some stadiums are run down a bit. But I'll guarantee you it's more exciting to watch than the NFL.

I never felt humiliated to be in the CFL. I think it's important, no matter the level, to play as if every game is the big-time.

I love playing almost any sport. If I'm driving around Natick and see a basketball game going in someone's driveway, I might stop and play.

Sometimes we'll play with lowered rims. Then it's not who scores the most points but who has the most dunks.

To me, sports is about competing. If you give it your all, you can handle the winning or losing.

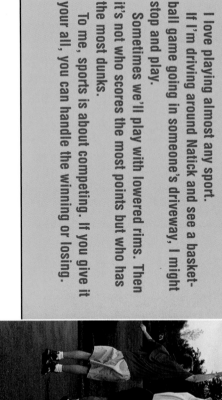

Doug set a CFL record with 6,619 passing yards his second year with the Lions and won his first of six CFL Most Outstanding Player awards.

I enjoyed most of my eight years playing in CFL—two in Vancouver, four in Calgary, and two in Toronto. The first year in Vancouver wasn't so great; we were 6–11–1. The next season, however, Darren joined the team and football became fun again.

My time playing on the same team with my brother didn't last long. My contract with B.C. was only two years. Calgary came calling with a record-setting CFL contract, and I became a Stampeder.

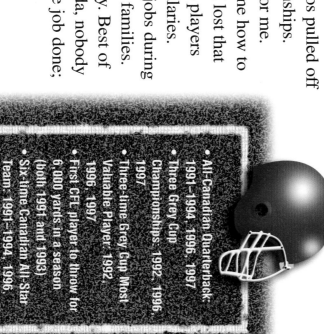

I went to Calgary hailed in the media as the Wayne Gretzky of the CFL. Expectations were high, and our team lived up to them by beating Winnipeg for the title.

The next two seasons ended in playoff losses, one at the hands of B.C. and Darren, who caught the game-winning touchdown pass against my team. His team went on to win the Grey Cup. I also endured a season in which I needed elbow surgery and faced the fear of my career ending, but I came back for the playoffs and my team lost to Baltimore in the Grey Cup.

After the 1985 season, the Calgary owner traded me to the Toronto Argonauts because he had financial trouble and could not afford to pay my salary.

The next two seasons our Argos pulled off back-to-back Grey Cup championships.

Those were special victories for me.

Playing in the CFL taught me how to enjoy playing football again. I lost that the first time in the NFL. CFL players don't have the egos and big salaries. Some players hold down real jobs during the season to provide for their families. CFL players are hungry to play. Best of all, in my eight years in Canada, nobody mentioned my height. I got the job done; that's all that mattered.

- All-Canadian Quarterback:
  1991–1994, 1996, 1997
- Three Grey Cup
  Championships: 1992, 1996,
  1997
- Three-time Grey Cup Most
  Valuable Player: 1992,
  1996, 1997
- First CFL player to throw for
  6,000 yards in a season
  (both 1991 and 1993)
- Six-time Canadian All-Star
  Team: 1991–1994, 1996,
  1997
- Six-time CFL Most
  Outstanding Player:
  1991–1994, 1996, 1997

Laurie and I have two children: our daughter Alexa and our son Dougie. Alexa is a great dancer and soccer player, and Dougie is a very special boy.

During my time in Canada, my family learned of an affliction that affected Dougie.

He seemed just as typical as our daughter Alexa. He talked in full sentences by the time he turned three. Then, mysteriously, he stopped talking and withdrew into his own world, a condition known as autism. The brain disorder turned back his mental development. So while his body grows, he's still one-and-a-half years old mentally.

Dougie is not as bad off as others with autism. He is the sweetest little guy. He always has a smile on his face and brings smiles to others who meet him.

Still, it has been devastating. He needs twenty-four-hour care for his special needs.

At first it was hard to take. You struggle with, "Why did this happen to Dougie?"

We don't know why. We know it's not fair, and we know it's nobody's fault.

Thanks to our faith, we accept and love Dougie for who he is. Still, we never give up hope that someone will find a cure someday.

After my second season in Toronto, I became a free agent. I would have been happy to finish my career in the CFL. But several NFL teams showed interest. Buffalo wanted me the most, so I decided to give the NFL another try. I took a huge pay cut to catch on with the Bills. Many writers and sports radio hosts blasted Buffalo for signing me. Laurie thought I was crazy to subject myself to such criticism again. A fair chance is all I wanted.

Shortly after signing me, the Bills acquired 6-foot-4 Rob Johnson from Jacksonville for a first-round pick and named him the starting quarterback going into the season.

Johnson did start, but a rib injury sidelined him early in the season. I stepped in and directed a pair of come-from-behind wins, including a 70-yard last-minute drive against Jacksonville that ended with me running a "blessed bootleg" in for a touchdown from the 1-yard line. That made us 5–3. Suddenly, I found myself riding a wave of support. People called it "Fluttemania." A cereal was even named after me: Flutie Flakes. Some of the money raised from the sale of the cereal goes toward my son's foundation for autism.

A tough regular-season loss at New England on two controversial calls cost us home-field advantage in the 1998 playoffs and paired us against the Dolphins in Miami in the first round.

In the final two minutes, we staged a near-miraculous comeback, scoring a field goal with 93 seconds left and recovering the onside kick. We drove to the Miami 5-yard line with 17 seconds left, down 24–17. But on the next play, my first receiver wasn't open, and I held the ball too long. A blind-side sack jarred the football from my hand. Miami recovered and ran out the clock.

Dolphins coach Jimmy Johnson, who coached the Miami Hurricanes when my Hail Mary pass beat them in 1984, threw a box of Flutie Flakes cereal on the locker room floor and stomped on it in celebration with his players. To me, they were disrepecting Dougie.

The Dolphins later apologized. I accepted the apology.

DOUGIE'S TEAM
DOUG FLUTIE JR. FOUNDATION FOR AUTISM

Falling five yards short is tough to swallow. Still, I felt our 10–7 season gave Bills fans hope, and I thought I proved what I could do.

Being around Dougie has a way of easing the pain of football losses. There are more important things than sports. In twenty years, games will be forgotten, but Dougie will still need special help.

My experiences in football have helped me face challenges head-on. Instead of feeling sorry for ourselves, Laurie and I wanted to do something about autism.

With my Bills' signing bonus, we started the Doug Flutie Jr. Foundation, which is a lifelong commitment to make a difference in the lives of autistic children and their families. The foundation surpassed the $1 million mark in funds raised in July 1999. We marked the milestone with a town-square party in Natick to thank all who donated time and money.

On Capitol Hill in 1999, Anthony Edwards (left) from the TV show "ER" and I asked the government to expand autism research.

Sales of Flutie Flakes have surpassed 2.1 million cereal boxes in 1999, helping the Doug Flutie Jr. Foundation top the $2 million mark in funds raised. The promotion also earned Doug the nickname "Flakes" among his Bills teammates.

The Flutie Brothers Band cut its second CD, entitled *The Flutie Gang Ramblin Scramblin Man* in 1999, with a portion of the profits going to the foundation.

LIMITED EDITION COLLECTOR'S BOX

PROVIDES 10 ESSENTIAL VITAMINS AND MINERALS

FLUTIE FLAKES

Frosted Corn Flakes

NET WT 20 OZ. (1 lb. 4 OZ) 567g

oundation for Autism
k Common.

The 1999 NFL season proved to be the strangest in years. Traditional winners were losers and long-time losers became winners. The Super Bowl was decided by one yard.

I started the season at quarterback, and we marched to a 10–5 mark with one regular-season game to play. Coach Wade Phillips rested me and started Johnson. It didn't matter if we won or lost. Johnson played well and I congratulated him.

But Coach Phillips shocked many, including me, by announcing Johnson would start our first-round playoff game against the Tennessee Titans.

A TV poll showed seventy percent of fans thought I deserved to start. In sports, the only vote that matters is the coach's. I had no choice but to accept it and be ready if the Bills needed me. Never had I faced a more frustrating situation in football—to be healthy and know I could help but not be allowed to play.

We'll never know if the outcome would have been different if I played. Johnson made some mistakes but led a gutsy last-minute drive to put us ahead by a field goal with thirteen seconds left.

Then, the Titans used a trick lateral play on the kickoff return for a game-winning touchdown to end our season. As the ball was in the air, I saw the wall of return players develop. Then time stood still as officials reviewed the play to rule if the lateral went forward (which is illegal) or not. It was the most eerie feeling as we waited for the decision. Finally, officials let the play stand.

Newspapers in Buffalo called the play "The Immaculate Deception." In Tennessee they called it "The Music City Miracle."

The last-minute loss added to the Bills' history of heartbreak, which includes four Super Bowl losses in four trips to the championship game. Although it's easy to explain such defeats as a curse, I don't believe in curses or bad luck.

I believe every season is a new chance, no matter what happened years before. Every game is a new chance, no matter what happened last week. Every play is a new chance, no matter what happened a second ago. To move forward, you must lock your negative past in the past.

It would be easy to be bitter about how the 1999 season ended for me personally.

But I don't have time for that. Bitterness only brings you down.

Like a teammate said after the Titan loss, each year we must be motivated to push ourselves to be our best—with no guarantees of what will happen in the end.

Despite Buffalo's history, I believe the Bills will win a Super Bowl, with or without me.

As long as I have time on my sports clock, I'll always be ready to make plays.

When my career is over, some might remember me as the short quarterback who played among the big boys. I hope you remember me as the quarterback who proved the experts wrong.

When someone tries to tackle your dream by saying "You'll never do it. . . . That's never been done. . . . That will never happen," just answer them like I do.

Tell them, "Never say never."